BATHFIRMATIONS

A UNIQUE APPROACH TO SUCCESS, WELL-BEING, AND FINANCIAL FREEDOM

S. "COACH" ATHELLI

Cover Sun Artwork and Back Cover Photo by:
Remy Athelli

Contents

Preface

Join the movement and not the BM kind! Using your time on the toilet productively. Although this book was created with the intention of a bathroom reader, BATHFIRMATIONS is quickly becoming a top seller in the motivation genre and obviously can be read anywhere. Personal word from me the author. I am not a writer by trade. I am just like you. I am another person looking for my own path to success and I know it will come. That being said, I am much more of a speaker than someone who can put down grammatically correct sentences on paper. This book is written the way I would talk to you and for your literary experts out there that may be cringing on my sentence structure, I have no apologies. I am not going to pretend to be someone I am not. See right there that last sentence was incorrect. Get over it! Once you do, you will not want to put this book down! Thank you for buying my book, It means the world to my family and I.

Be blessed!
Coach Athelli

Introduction

Welcome to the most unexpected journey to success you will ever embark on—right from the comfort of your own bathroom! Pooping with Purpose. We are about to dive headfirst into a topic that is both hilariously unconventional and surprisingly effective. Yes, you read that right—we are talking about using affirmations while doing your business on the porcelain throne! Think about it! When you are doing your business in the restroom, that time is typically the most quality undistracted time most people get during their day. No one is trying to talk to you and command your attention. During this time, even if just a few minutes a day, you can use it positively without judgement to change your life.

Now, you might be wondering: "Affirmations in the bathroom? Really?" Absolutely! Because let us face it, some of the best ideas come to us while we're sitting on the toilet, right? Also in new scientific studies, the first 30 minutes of waking up are the most influential on your mindset, and about 98% of people in the world go to the restroom as one of those activities to start the day. So instead of sabotaging your day with social media, or phone video games, why not use that time to supercharge our mindset and set ourselves up for success? Sabotage or supercharge. The choice is yours.

In this book, we are going to explore how reciting affirmations while going poo can lead to amazing positive benefits. From boosting your confidence and productivity to fostering mindfulness and clarity, you will be amazed at the transformative power of these simple yet powerful statements. Most will see results in less than a week. In a few months, positive thoughts lead to positive actions, and within the year positive actions lead to AMAZING results. This will 100% change your life.

The great author and successful conglomerate T Harv Eker said it best. "Do you want to be rich? Or? Are you committed to being rich?"

Wanting something is so much different than committing to something. The choice is yours!

So, whether you're a seasoned affirmations enthusiast or a skeptical newbie, get ready to commit to joining the BATHFIRMATIONS movement and become a true champion of the bathroom affirmations revolution. It is time to flush away negativity, embrace positivity, and poop your way to success like never before! Get ready to laugh, learn, and transform your bathroom routine into a powerhouse of productivity and positivity. Let's do this!

CHAPTER 1

RISE WITH PURPOSE

THE FIRST 30 MINUTES OF WAKING UP
ARE THE MOST INFLUENTIAL ON YOUR
MIND, BODY, AND SOUL

Read that again!

THE FIRST 30 MINUTES OF WAKING UP
ARE THE MOST INFLUENTIAL ON YOUR
MIND, BODY, AND SOUL

The First 30 minutes of what you put in your mind each day are among the most important. In the grand symphony of life, the first notes of the day are crucial. They set the tone, dictate the rhythm, and pave the way for the melodies that will follow. Such is the power of rising with purpose.

Purpose is the guiding star that illuminates our journey through life. It gives meaning to our actions, direction to our endeavors, and clarity to our decisions. And it all begins with those sacred moments upon waking, where the canvas of a new day lies blank, waiting to be painted with intention.

As the first light of dawn pierces the darkness, it beckons us to awaken not just our bodies, but also our spirits. It calls us to rise with a sense of purpose, a sense of mission that transcends the mundane and ignites the soul.

But how do we cultivate purpose in those precious first moments of wakefulness? It starts with intention. Before even opening our eyes, we can take a moment to set a clear intention for the day ahead. This intention can be as simple as affirming our commitment to living with gratitude, kindness, or courage. Or it can be as specific as visualizing ourselves achieving a particular goal or milestone.

By anchoring our minds with purpose, we create a mental roadmap that guides our actions and choices throughout the day. We become less reactive to external circumstances and more proactive in shaping our destiny. Challenges transform into opportunities for growth, setbacks become steppingstones to success, and every moment becomes infused with meaning and significance.

Rising with purpose also means aligning our actions with our values and aspirations. It requires us to ask ourselves: What truly matters to me? What am I enthusiastic about? What legacy do I want to leave behind? By clarifying our values and priorities, we can make conscious decisions that honor our deepest desires and aspirations.

Moreover, rising with purpose empowers us to live authentically and wholeheartedly. It encourages us to pursue our passions, follow our dreams, and embrace our unique gifts and talents. It reminds us that life is not just about achieving external success or accolades but about living with integrity, authenticity, and meaning.

Ultimately, rising with purpose is an ongoing practice—a daily commitment to living with intention and integrity. It requires us to cultivate self-awareness, listen to the whispers of our hearts, and follow the path that resonates with our deepest truths. And it all begins with those first 30 minutes of waking up, where the seeds of purpose are planted and nurtured with care and intention.

In the end, rising with purpose is not just about what we do but who we are becoming. It is about embracing our inherent worth and dignity, acknowledging our interconnectedness with all beings, and contributing our unique gifts to the tapestry of life. So let us rise each morning with purpose, passion, and presence, for in doing so, we illuminate the world with the light of our souls.

CHAPTER 2

PRACTICE GRATITUDE - CULTIVATING AN ATTITUDE OF APPRECIATION

In the hustle and bustle of modern life, it is easy to overlook the simple blessings that surround us each day. Yet, taking a moment to pause and express gratitude can profoundly impact our well-being and success. Chapter 2 delves deeper into the practice of gratitude, exploring its transformative power and offering practical tips for incorporating it into your morning routine.

Gratitude is more than just saying "thank you" or acknowledging the good things in our lives; it is a mindset, a way of seeing the world with appreciation and abundance. Research in positive psychology has shown that cultivating gratitude can lead to a host of benefits, including improved physical health, enhanced mental well-being, and increased resilience in the face of adversity.

Upon waking, before the demands of the day clamor for attention, the first 30 minutes offer a sacred opportunity to cultivate gratitude. It is a time to reflect on the blessings that often go unnoticed amidst the chaos of daily life. Whether it is the roof over our heads, the warmth of sunlight streaming through the window, or the love of family and friends, there is always something to be thankful for.

One of the most powerful aspects of practicing gratitude is its ability to shift our perspective from scarcity to abundance. In a world where we are bombarded with messages of what we lack or need to achieve happiness, gratitude reminds us of the richness and abundance that already exists in our lives. By focusing on what we have rather than what we lack, we cultivate a sense of contentment and fulfillment that permeates every aspect of our being.

Gratitude affirmations play a significant role in shaping our mindset, attitudes, and overall well-being. Here are some key reasons highlighting their importance:

Positive Mindset: Gratitude affirmations help cultivate a positive outlook on life by focusing our attention on the blessings and abundance that surround us. By repeating affirmations that express appreciation and thankfulness, we train our minds to see the good in every situation, even amidst challenges.

Shift in Perspective: Affirmations have the power to shift our perspective from one of lack and scarcity to one of abundance and fulfillment. Instead of dwelling on what we don't have or haven't achieved, gratitude affirmations remind us of the richness and abundance that already exists in our lives, fostering a sense of contentment and satisfaction.

Rewiring the Subconscious Mind: Affirmations work by reprogramming the subconscious mind with positive beliefs and attitudes. When we consistently repeat gratitude affirmations, we create new neural pathways that reinforce feelings of appreciation and gratitude, replacing old patterns of negativity and dissatisfaction.

Increased Resilience: Gratitude affirmations can boost resilience and emotional strength, enabling us to bounce back more quickly from setbacks and adversity. By focusing on the positive aspects of our lives, even during challenging times, we build inner resilience and fortitude that help us navigate life's ups and downs with grace and courage.

Enhanced Well-being: Research has shown that practicing gratitude has numerous benefits for mental, emotional, and physical health. Gratitude affirmations contribute to this by promoting feelings of happiness, optimism, and overall well-being. They can reduce stress, anxiety, and depression, while also improving sleep quality and fostering stronger relationships.

Manifestation of Desires: Affirmations are a powerful tool for manifestation, as they help align our thoughts, beliefs, and actions with our desires and goals. When we express gratitude for the things we wish to attract into our lives, we send a powerful message to the universe that we are ready to receive them. This positive energy can accelerate the manifestation process and bring our desires into reality more swiftly.

Improved Self-esteem: Gratitude affirmations can boost self-esteem and self-worth by affirming our inherent value and worthiness. When we acknowledge and appreciate our strengths, talents, and achievements, we develop a deeper sense of self-confidence and self-assurance that empowers us to pursue our goals with conviction and courage.

In summary, gratitude affirmations are a valuable tool for fostering a positive mindset, cultivating resilience, and enhancing overall well-being. By incorporating them into our daily routine, we can harness the transformative power of gratitude to create a life filled with joy, abundance, and fulfillment.

CHAPTER 3

HYDRATE AND ENERGIZE - FUELING YOUR BODY AND MIND FOR SUCCESS

The first 30 minutes upon waking are a crucial window of opportunity to nourish and energize your body and mind for the day ahead. In Chapter 3, we delve into the importance of hydration and nutrition in optimizing your morning routine and maximizing your potential for success.

Hydration is fundamental to human health and well-being, yet it's a component of self-care that often gets overlooked, especially in the rush of the morning routine. After a night of sleep, during which the body undergoes a process of repair and rejuvenation, it's essential to replenish lost fluids and jumpstart your metabolism.

Water is the elixir of life, and drinking a glass of it as soon as you wake up can work wonders for your body. Not only does it rehydrate you after hours of sleep-induced dehydration, but it also kickstarts your metabolism and helps flush out toxins accumulated overnight. Hydrating first thing in the morning sets the tone for the rest of the day, priming your body for optimal functioning and performance.

But hydration isn't just about drinking water; it's also about incorporating hydrating foods and beverages into your morning routine. Fresh fruits and vegetables, such as watermelon, cucumbers, and oranges, are excellent sources of hydration and provide essential vitamins, minerals, and antioxidants to support overall health and vitality. Herbal teas and coconut water are other hydrating options that offer additional benefits for digestion, immunity, and hydration.

In addition to hydration, nutrition plays a crucial role in fueling your body and mind for success. Breakfast is often touted as the most important meal of the day, and for good reason. It provides the essential nutrients and energy your body needs to function optimally throughout the day, including carbohydrates for fuel, protein for muscle repair and growth, and healthy fats for sustained energy and brain function.

When planning your morning meal, aim for a balanced combination of macronutrients to keep you feeling satisfied and energized until your next meal. Incorporate whole foods such as whole grains, lean proteins, healthy fats, and plenty of fruits and vegetables to provide a diverse array of nutrients and promote satiety.

Incorporating protein-rich foods into your breakfast is particularly important, as protein helps stabilize blood sugar levels, promote muscle repair and growth, and keep you feeling full and satisfied throughout the morning. Incorporate sources such as eggs, Greek yogurt, tofu, nuts, seeds, and lean meats or plant-based alternatives into your morning meal to support your body's needs.

In addition to hydration and nutrition, the first 30 minutes of waking up are an opportune time to engage in activities that energize and invigorate your body and mind. Whether it's a quick workout, a morning stretch, or a few minutes of deep breathing exercises, incorporating movement and mindfulness into your morning routine sets a positive tone for the day ahead.

Exercise has been shown to boost mood, increase energy levels, and enhance cognitive function, making it an ideal way to kickstart your day. Even just a few minutes of moderate-intensity exercise can have significant benefits for physical and mental well-being. Whether it's a brisk walk around the neighborhood, a short yoga flow, or a quick bodyweight workout, find a form of exercise that you enjoy and can easily incorporate into your morning routine.

In addition to exercise, mindfulness practices such as meditation, deep breathing exercises, and gratitude journaling can help calm the mind, reduce stress, and enhance focus and concentration. Taking a few moments to center yourself in the present moment can set a positive tone for the rest of the day, helping you approach challenges with clarity and resilience.

By prioritizing hydration, nutrition, and mindful movement in the first 30 minutes of waking up, you set yourself up for success by nourishing your body and mind and priming yourself for a productive and fulfilling day ahead. Remember that small, consistent actions add up over time, so prioritize your morning routine and watch as it transforms your health, happiness, and overall well-being.

CHAPTER 4

ENGAGE IN MINDFULNESS AND CULTIVATE BALANCE WITH VITALITY FOR SUCCESS

In the rush of modern life, it's easy to get caught up in the hustle and bustle of daily tasks and responsibilities, often neglecting our own well-being in the process. However, the first 30 minutes upon waking offer a precious opportunity to prioritize self-care and set a positive tone for the day ahead. In Chapters 4 and 5, we explore the importance of engaging in mindfulness and movement to cultivate balance, vitality, and success in all areas of life.

Mindfulness, the practice of being fully present and aware of the present moment, has gained widespread popularity in recent years for its numerous benefits for mental, emotional, and physical health. Incorporating mindfulness into your morning routine can help reduce stress, enhance focus and concentration, and promote a sense of calm and inner peace.

One powerful way to cultivate mindfulness in the first 30 minutes of waking up is through meditation. Taking just a few minutes to sit quietly, focus on your breath, and observe your thoughts and sensations can have profound effects on your overall well-being. Meditation helps calm the mind, reduce stress, and cultivate a sense of inner peace and clarity that sets a positive tone for the rest of the day.

In addition to meditation, there are many other mindfulness practices you can incorporate into your morning routine, such as deep breathing exercises, mindful eating, and gratitude journaling. These practices help anchor you in the present moment, cultivate a sense of gratitude and appreciation, and foster a positive mindset that empowers you to face whatever challenges may arise throughout the day.

As you engage in mindfulness practices, it's also important to move your body and incorporate physical activity into your morning routine. Exercise not only helps improve physical health and fitness but also has numerous benefits for mental and emotional well-being. Moving your body in the morning helps boost energy levels, improve mood, and enhance cognitive function, setting a positive tone for the rest of the day.

There are many ways to incorporate movement into your morning routine, depending on your preferences and fitness level. Whether it's a brisk walk, a yoga session, or a quick workout, find an activity that you enjoy and that leaves you feeling energized and invigorated. Even just a few minutes of movement can have significant benefits for your overall well-being.

In addition to mindfulness and movement, daily affirmations are another powerful tool for cultivating a positive mindset and setting the tone for success. Affirmations are positive statements that help reprogram your subconscious mind and reinforce beliefs and attitudes conducive to achieving your goals and aspirations.

When done consistently, affirmations can help boost self-confidence, increase resilience, and enhance motivation and focus. They help shift your mindset from one of limitation and self-doubt to one of empowerment and possibility, empowering you to overcome obstacles and pursue your dreams with passion and determination.

Incorporating affirmations into your morning routine is a simple yet effective way to set a positive tone for the day ahead. Whether you write them down, recite them aloud, or simply repeat them silently to yourself, affirmations can help anchor you in a positive mindset and create a sense of alignment and purpose that propels you forward toward your goals.

Here are some examples of affirmations you can incorporate into your morning routine:

"I am capable of achieving anything I set my mind to."

"I radiate confidence, positivity, and optimism."

"I am worthy of love, success, and abundance in all areas of my life."

"I embrace challenges as opportunities for growth and learning."

"I am grateful for the abundance of blessings in my life, both big and small."

"I trust in my ability to overcome obstacles and create the life of my dreams."

"I am surrounded by love, support, and positivity."

"I am filled with energy, vitality, and enthusiasm for life."

"I deserve all the happiness, success, and fulfillment that life has to offer."

As you incorporate mindfulness, movement, and affirmations into your morning routine, remember that consistency is key. Set aside dedicated time each morning to prioritize self-care and personal growth and watch as these practices transform your life from the inside out. By nurturing your body, mind, and spirit in the first 30 minutes of waking up, you set a powerful foundation for success and well-being that resonates throughout the rest of your day.

CHAPTER 5

SETTING THE INTENTION - HARNESSING THE POWER OF PURPOSE FOR SUCCESS

In the tapestry of life, intention serves as the guiding thread that weaves our dreams into reality. In this chapter we explore the profound significance of setting intentions in the first 30 minutes of waking up and how it can shape the trajectory of our day, our goals, and ultimately, our lives.

Setting intentions is more than just wishful thinking or setting vague goals; it is about consciously directing our thoughts, actions, and energy toward a specific outcome or desired state of being. When we set intentions, we clarify our vision, focus our attention, and align our actions with our deepest desires and values.

The first 30 minutes upon waking offer a unique opportunity to set the tone for the day ahead by consciously choosing our intentions. As we transition from the realm of dreams to the realm of waking reality, we have a chance to pause, reflect, and set the course for how we want to show up in the world.

But what exactly does it mean to set intentions, and how can we do so effectively in the first moments of waking up? Here are some key principles to keep in mind:

Clarity: Take time to clarify what you genuinely want to manifest or experience in your life. What are your goals, aspirations, and priorities? What qualities or virtues do you want to embody? By getting clear on your intentions, you create a blueprint for success and align your energy with your highest vision for yourself.

Focus: Once you have clarified your intentions, focus your attention and energy on them with unwavering commitment and dedication. Visualize yourself already living your intentions as if they were already true. Feel the emotions associated with achieving your goals and let them permeate every fiber of your being.

Positivity: Frame your intentions in a positive light, focusing on what you want to attract or create rather than what you want to avoid or eliminate. Positive intentions carry a higher vibration and are more likely to manifest into reality. Instead of saying, "I want to avoid stress," say, "I intend to cultivate inner peace and serenity."

Surrender: Release attachment to the outcome and trust in the process of manifestation. While setting intentions is a powerful tool for creating change, it's important to surrender control and allow the universe to work its magic in its own time and way. Trust that the universe has your back and is conspiring in your favor.

So how can you incorporate intention-setting into your morning routine? Here are some practical strategies to try:

Morning Rituals: Create a morning ritual that incorporates intention-setting as a vital component. This could include practices such as meditation, visualization, journaling, or affirmations. Dedicate time each morning to connect with your intentions and anchor yourself in the vision of your highest self.

Affirmations: Use affirmations to reinforce your intentions and program your subconscious mind for success. Repeat positive affirmations that align with your intentions, such as "I am confident, capable, and worthy of success" or "I attract abundance and prosperity into my life with ease."

Visualization: Engage in visualization exercises to vividly imagine yourself living your intentions. Close your eyes and picture yourself already embodying the qualities or experiences you desire. Use all of your senses to make the visualization as real and immersive as possible.

Gratitude: Cultivate an attitude of gratitude for the fulfillment of your intentions, even before they have manifested into reality. Express gratitude for the abundance and blessings already present in your life, as well as for the infinite possibilities that lie ahead.

Action: Take inspired action toward your intentions each day, no matter how small or incremental. Break down your goals into manageable steps and commit to taking consistent action toward their realization. Trust that each step you take brings you closer to your desired outcome.

By setting intentions in the first 30 minutes of waking up, you take ownership of your life and consciously direct your energy toward the realization of your goals and dreams. By aligning your thoughts, beliefs, and actions with your intentions, you harness the power of purpose to create a life of meaning, fulfillment, and success.

CHAPTER 6

PRACTICE VISUALIZATION - MANIFESTING SUCCESS IN THE FIRST 30 MINUTES OF YOUR DAY

In the ethereal realm between dreaming and wakefulness, lies a potent tool for shaping our reality - visualization. Let's delve into the transformative power of visualization within the first 30 minutes of waking up, elucidating how this practice can harness the subconscious mind for success, making aspirations tangible and attainable.

Visualization is not merely a passive act of daydreaming; it's a deliberate and focused mental rehearsal of desired outcomes. When we engage in visualization, we create vivid mental images of ourselves achieving our goals, embodying the feelings of success, and living our most fulfilling lives. By repeatedly visualizing our desired outcomes with clarity and intention, we program our subconscious minds to align our thoughts, beliefs, and actions with those visions, thus paving the way for their realization.

The first 30 minutes of waking up offer a fertile ground for practicing visualization, as the mind is in a relaxed and receptive state, making it more susceptible to suggestion and imagery. By incorporating visualization into our morning routine, we can set a positive tone for the day ahead, align our energy with our goals, and cultivate a sense of empowerment and confidence that propels us toward success.

So, how can we effectively practice visualization within the first 30 minutes of waking up? Let's explore some practical strategies and techniques to harness the power of visualization for manifesting success:

Clear Intentions: Before engaging in visualization, it's essential to have clear intentions about what you want to manifest in your life. Take time to identify your goals, aspirations, and desires, and distill them into concise, specific statements. Whether it's achieving career milestones, cultivating fulfilling relationships, or improving health and well-being, clarity of intention is the first step toward effective visualization.

Relaxation Techniques: Begin your visualization practice by inducing a state of deep relaxation. Find a comfortable position, close your eyes, and take several deep breaths to center yourself and quiet the mind. Progressive muscle relaxation, guided imagery, or mindfulness meditation can help facilitate relaxation and prepare the mind for visualization.

Vivid Imagery: Once in a relaxed state, begin to visualize your desired outcomes with vivid detail and clarity. Imagine yourself achieving your goals with all your senses engaged - see, hear, feel, smell, and even taste the experience as if it were happening in real-time. Visualize every aspect of the scenario, from the sights and sounds to the emotions and sensations associated with success.

Positive Affirmations: Complement your visualization practice with positive affirmations that reinforce your desired outcomes. Repeat affirmations that affirm your belief in your ability to achieve your goals, such as "I am capable, confident, and deserving of success" or "I attract abundance and opportunities into my life effortlessly." By combining visualization with affirmations, you amplify the impact of both practices and further align your subconscious mind with your goals.

Emotional Connection: Engage your emotions in your visualization practice by embodying the feelings of achievement, fulfillment, and joy associated with your desired outcomes. Allow yourself to fully immerse in the experience and experience the emotions as if they were already true. The more emotionally invested you are in your visualization, the more potent its effects will be in shaping your reality.

Repetition and Consistency: Practice visualization consistently, ideally incorporating it into your morning routine within the first 30 minutes of waking up. Repetition is key to ingraining new beliefs and patterns into the subconscious mind, so make visualization a daily habit and revisit your visions regularly. Over time, you'll notice subtle shifts in your thoughts, behaviors, and circumstances as your subconscious mind aligns with your visualized outcomes.

Gratitude and Surrender: Conclude your visualization practice with an attitude of gratitude and surrender, expressing thanks for the manifestation of your desired outcomes and releasing attachment to the timing or specifics of how they will unfold. Trust in the process of manifestation and surrender control to the universe, knowing that your visions are being held and supported by a higher power.

By integrating visualization into your morning routine, you set a powerful intention for the day ahead and lay the groundwork for the manifestation of your goals and desires. Visualization primes your subconscious mind for success, making your aspirations more tangible and attainable. As you consistently engage in visualization within the first 30 minutes of waking up, you'll find yourself becoming more aligned with your goals, more confident in your abilities, and more attuned to the opportunities that arise to bring your visions to fruition.

Incorporating visualization into your morning routine is a potent way to harness the power of your subconscious mind and accelerate your journey toward success and fulfillment. So, as you greet each new day, take a moment to close your eyes, envision your dreams coming true, and step into the reality you desire with confidence and conviction. The power to manifest your dreams lies within you - harness it, visualize it, and watch as your reality transforms before your eyes.

CHAPTER 7

CONNECT WITH LOVED ONES

As the first rays of sunlight gently filter through the window, the morning offers a sacred opportunity to connect with loved ones and express gratitude for their presence in our lives. This chapter invites us to pause and acknowledge the importance of nurturing relationships, fostering emotional well-being, and strengthening our support networks.

Make a plan of action after your first 30 minutes and take a moment to reach out to loved ones, whether through a heartfelt conversation, a text message, or a note of gratitude. Express appreciation for their support, love, and companionship, and let them know how much they mean to you. By nurturing relationships and fostering connections, we deepen our sense of belonging and create a supportive network that uplifts and sustains us through life's challenges.

Connection is not just a fleeting interaction; it's a lifeline that nourishes our souls and enriches our lives. When we take time to connect with loved ones, we strengthen the bonds of friendship and family, cultivate empathy and compassion, and foster a sense of belonging and community. In the tapestry of life, relationships are the threads that weave our experiences together, creating a mosaic of love, laughter, and shared memories.

CHAPTER 8

SEIZE THE DAY

With purpose, gratitude, and mindfulness as our allies, this chapter urges us to seize the day with confidence and enthusiasm. It encourages us to approach each task and challenge with a positive mindset and a sense of purpose, leveraging the first 30 minutes of our day to set the stage for success and empower ourselves to achieve greatness.

As we greet each new day with intention and purpose, we affirm our commitment to living a life of meaning and fulfillment. We embrace the opportunities that lie ahead with open hearts and open minds, knowing that each moment is a chance to learn, grow, and evolve. With purpose as our compass, we navigate the complexities of life with clarity and conviction, staying true to our values and aspirations.

By seizing the day, we harness the full potential of each moment, making the most of our time and energy to pursue our goals and dreams. We approach challenges with resilience and determination, knowing that every obstacle is an opportunity for growth and transformation. With gratitude as our guide, we appreciate the beauty and abundance that surrounds us, finding joy in the simple pleasures of life and celebrating our achievements along the way.

Combining the information, we recognize that connection and purpose are the cornerstones of a fulfilling and successful life. By nurturing relationships and fostering connections with loved ones, we create a support network that sustains us through life's ups and downs. By seizing the day with purpose and intention, we set the stage for success and empower ourselves to live authentically and passionately.

Incorporating these practices into our morning routine, we create a foundation for success and well-being that resonates throughout the rest of the day. As we connect with loved ones, express gratitude, and embrace opportunity, we cultivate a sense of purpose and fulfillment that enriches every aspect of our lives. So as you greet each new day, take a moment to connect with loved ones, seize the day with purpose and enthusiasm, and embrace the possibilities that lie ahead. The journey of life is yours to navigate - embrace it with open arms and a grateful heart.

CHAPTER 9

NEGATIVE INFLUENCES IN THE FIRST 30 MINUTES OF WAKING UP EACH DAY.

The harmful effects of using social media, electronics, and television in the first 30 minutes of waking up as part of a daily routine can significantly impact our success in various ways. Here are some of the detrimental effects:

Mental Clutter and Distraction: Scrolling through social media feeds, checking emails, or watching television first thing in the morning can flood our minds with unnecessary information and distractions. This mental clutter can make it challenging to focus on our priorities, set clear goals, and establish a positive mindset for the day ahead.

Negative Comparison and Self-Esteem Issues: Social media platforms are often filled with carefully curated images and highlight reels that can foster feelings of comparison, inadequacy, and low self-esteem. Constant exposure to these idealized representations of others' lives can erode our self-confidence and undermine our belief in our own abilities and worth, hindering our success.

Reduced Productivity and Focus: Engaging with electronics and television in the morning can derail our productivity and focus, making it difficult to tackle important tasks and projects. The passive consumption of content on these platforms can lead to procrastination, time-wasting, and a lack of motivation to pursue our goals with purpose and determination.

Increased Stress and Anxiety: The barrage of information and stimuli from social media, emails, and television can trigger stress and anxiety responses in the body and mind. Constant exposure to negative news stories, sensationalized content, or conflict-ridden social media interactions can heighten feelings of overwhelm, anxiety, and uncertainty, detracting from our ability to approach challenges with clarity and resilience.

Disrupted Sleep Patterns: Using electronics such as smartphones, tablets, or televisions before bed and upon waking can disrupt our natural sleep-wake cycles and negatively impact the quality of our sleep. The blue light emitted by screens can interfere with the production of melatonin, the hormone responsible for regulating sleep, leading to difficulty falling asleep and experiencing restorative rest. Poor sleep quality can impair cognitive function, mood regulation, and overall well-being, ultimately undermining our ability to succeed in our endeavors.

Decreased Mindfulness and Presence: Engaging with social media, electronics, and television in the morning can detract from our ability to be fully present and mindful in the moment. Instead of savoring the quiet moments of reflection and setting positive intentions for the day ahead, we may find ourselves mindlessly scrolling through feeds or passively consuming content, missing out on opportunities for personal growth, connection, and self-discovery.

In summary, the use of social media, electronics, and television in the first 30 minutes of waking up can have harmful effects on our mental, emotional, and physical well-being, ultimately impeding our success. Believe it or not, this habit is now being statistically shown to be a leading catalyst in destroying relationships as well. Use of electronics and social media first thing in the morning creates so much subliminal negative self-energy, and that energy will affect anyone who interacts with you as well. By minimizing exposure to these distractions and prioritizing activities that nourish our mind, body, and spirit, we can reclaim control over our mornings and set ourselves up for a day of purpose, productivity, and fulfillment.

In Summary here are some of the main contributors **that are harmful** in the first 30 minutes of waking up:

Checking Social Media: Scrolling through social media feeds can lead to comparison, feelings of inadequacy, and distractions that hinder productivity and focus for the rest of the day.

Reading Work Emails: Engaging with work-related emails first thing in the morning can trigger stress and anxiety, making it difficult to establish a positive mindset and approach the day with clarity and resilience.

Watching News or Negative Content: Exposing oneself to negative news stories or sensationalized content can lead to feelings of overwhelm, anxiety, and pessimism, detracting from the ability to cultivate a positive outlook and tackle challenges with optimism and determination.

Checking Text Messages: Responding to text messages or notifications from friends, family, or colleagues can disrupt the morning routine and divert attention away from setting intentions and priorities for the day ahead. Family and those you love are vitally important, so for this one, just make a plan to reach out to family after your 30 minutes of self-time.

Procrastinating or Snoozing: Giving in to the temptation to procrastinate or hit the snooze button repeatedly can delay the start of the day, leading to rushed mornings, increased stress, and decreased productivity. The harmful effects of the Snooze button can be its own book. This one is tough, and even as the author I still struggle with this.

Engaging in Negative Self-Talk: Starting the day with self-criticism, doubt, or negative self-talk can undermine confidence, motivation, and self-belief, making it harder to pursue goals and overcome obstacles with resilience and determination.

Skipping Hydration and Nutrition: Neglecting to hydrate or nourish the body with a healthy breakfast can lead to low energy levels, poor concentration, and decreased productivity throughout the day.

In summary, activities such as checking social media, reading work emails, consuming negative content, responding to text messages, procrastinating, engaging in negative self-talk, and skipping hydration and nutrition can negatively affect success when exposed in the first 30 minutes of waking up. By avoiding these distractions and prioritizing activities that promote well-being, mindfulness, and positivity, individuals can set themselves up for a successful and fulfilling day ahead.

CHAPTER 10

BENEFITS OF AFFIRMATIONS

And so we finally get to one of the very best ways to start each day.

Reciting affirmations in the first 30 minutes of each day can offer numerous benefits for mental, emotional, and physical well-being. Here are some of the key advantages:

Sets a Positive Tone: Starting the day with affirmations helps set a positive tone for the rest of the day. Affirmations are positive statements that affirm our beliefs, values, and goals. By reciting affirmations in the morning, we prime our minds to focus on what we want to achieve and cultivate a mindset of positivity and optimism.

Boosts Confidence and Self-Esteem: Affirmations can help boost confidence and self-esteem by reinforcing positive beliefs about ourselves. When we repeat affirmations that affirm our strengths, capabilities, and worth, we internalize these messages and develop a greater sense of self-assurance and self-belief.

Fosters Resilience: Affirmations can foster resilience by encouraging us to focus on our strengths and abilities rather than dwelling on limitations or setbacks. By affirming our resilience and ability to overcome challenges, we cultivate a mindset of perseverance and determination that helps us navigate obstacles with greater ease and grace.

Promotes Goal Achievement: Affirmations can help align our thoughts, beliefs, and actions with our goals and aspirations. By repeating affirmations that reflect our goals and desired outcomes, we program our subconscious mind to work toward their realization. This can increase motivation, focus, and commitment to taking consistent action toward our goals.

Reduces Stress and Anxiety: Affirmations can help reduce stress and anxiety by promoting feelings of calm, relaxation, and inner peace. When we recite affirmations that affirm our ability to cope with stress and maintain a positive outlook, we activate the body's relaxation response and counteract the effects of stress hormones.

Enhances Mindfulness and Presence: Affirmations can enhance mindfulness and presence by grounding us in the present moment and fostering awareness of our thoughts and emotions. When we recite affirmations mindfully, we cultivate a deeper connection to ourselves and our inner wisdom, enabling us to navigate life with greater clarity and intention.

Improves Self-Talk: Affirmations can help improve self-talk by replacing negative or self-critical thoughts with positive, empowering ones. When we consciously choose to focus on affirmations that uplift and inspire us, we create a more supportive internal dialogue that fuels confidence, motivation, and self-compassion.

Overall, reciting affirmations in the first 30 minutes of each day can have profound effects on our mindset, outlook, and overall well-being. By incorporating affirmations into our morning routine, we cultivate a positive mindset, boost confidence, foster resilience, promote goal achievement, reduce stress and anxiety, enhance mindfulness, and improve self-talk. As a result, we set ourselves up for success and approach each day with greater clarity, purpose, and optimism.

CHAPTER 11

DAILY AFFIRMATIONS

You are encouraged to flip through this section randomly while you sit in the bathroom or when you first wake up. We will leave a few blank pages at the end of the book, so you can write down your favorite affirmations. Affirmations are categorized. Find and highlight your favorite ones. If able it is best to read these aloud, for as when you speak, there is a vibration associated with the affirmation that helps it ring true to yourself and to your memory.

Note there are some affirmations intentionally repeated, and this is with scientific reason. Affirmations are much more effective when read, written, or spoken multiple times.

These Affirmations provide a comprehensive framework for self-improvement and empowerment.

Every day, I grow stronger and more resilient.

I radiate confidence and positivity.

My potential is limitless.

I am worthy of love and respect.
I attract abundance into my life effortlessly.

I am in control of my thoughts and emotions.

Challenges are opportunities for growth and learning.

I trust in my ability to overcome obstacles.

I deserve happiness and success.

I am surrounded by love and support.

I am enough just as I am.

I embrace change and adapt with ease.

My actions align with my goals and values.
I forgive myself for past mistakes and move forward with grace.

I am constantly evolving and improving.

I am confident in my abilities and talents.

I am the architect of my own destiny.

I am at peace with who I am.

I believe in my ability to achieve my dreams.

I am capable of creating the life I desire.

I am aligned with the universe and its abundance.

I attract positive, like-minded people into my life.

I am at peace with my past and excited for my future.

I am worthy of all the good things life has to offer.

I trust myself to make the right decisions.

I am filled with gratitude for all that I have.

I am open to receiving love and abundance.

I release all fears and doubts that hold me back.

I am becoming the best version of myself each day.

I trust in the process of life.

I am a magnet for miracles.

I am confident in my ability to manifest my dreams.

I am deserving of all the love and joy in the world.

I am powerful beyond measure.

I am courageous and willing to take risks.

I am creating the life of my dreams with every choice I make.
I am open to receiving all the blessings of the universe.

I am confident in my ability to succeed.

I am grateful for all the abundance in my life.

I am attracting positive energy into my life.

I am capable of overcoming any challenge that comes my way.

I am confident in my ability to overcome challenges.

I am worthy of love, happiness, and success.

I am a magnet for positivity and prosperity.
I am open to receiving all the abundance of the universe.

I am attracting positive energy into my life.

I am confident in my ability to manifest my dreams.

I am worthy of all the blessings coming my way.

I am open to receiving love and abundance.

I trust myself to make the right decisions.

I am filled with gratitude for all that I have.

I am becoming the best version of myself each day.

I trust in the process of life.

I am a magnet for miracles.

I am confident in my ability to achieve my dreams.

I am deserving of all the love and joy in the world.

I am powerful beyond measure.

I am courageous and willing to take risks.

I am creating the life of my dreams with every choice I make.

I am open to receiving all the blessings of the universe.

I am confident in my ability to succeed.

I am grateful for all the abundance in my life.

I am attracting positive energy into my life.

I am capable of overcoming any challenge that comes my way.

I am confident in my ability to overcome challenges.

I am worthy of love, happiness, and success.

I am a magnet for positivity and prosperity.

I am open to receiving all the abundance of the universe.
I am attracting positive energy into my life.

I am confident in my ability to manifest my dreams.

I am worthy of all the blessings coming my way.

I am open to receiving love and abundance.

I trust myself to make the right decisions.

I am filled with gratitude for all that I have.

I am becoming the best version of myself each day.

I trust in the process of life.

I am a magnet for miracles.
I am confident in my ability to achieve my dreams.

I am deserving of all the love and joy in the world.

I am powerful beyond measure.

I am courageous and willing to take risks.

I am creating the life of my dreams with every choice I make.

I am open to receiving all the blessings of the universe.

I am confident in my ability to succeed.

I am grateful for all the abundance in my life.
I am attracting positive energy into my life.

I am capable of overcoming any challenge that comes my way.

I am confident in my ability to overcome challenges.

I am worthy of love, happiness, and success.

I am a magnet for positivity and prosperity.

I am open to receiving all the abundance of the universe.

I am attracting positive energy into my life.

I am confident in my ability to manifest my dreams.
I am worthy of all the blessings coming my way.

I am open to receiving love and abundance.

I trust myself to make the right decisions.

I am filled with gratitude for all that I have.

I am becoming the best version of myself each day.

I trust in the process of life.

These affirmations can help reinforce a positive self-image and cultivate self-love and confidence daily.

I love and accept myself unconditionally.

I am confident in my own skin.

I embrace my unique qualities and talents.

I radiate beauty from within.

I am worthy of love and respect.

My imperfections make me unique and beautiful.

I am enough just as I am.

I celebrate my strengths and weaknesses.
I am confident in expressing my true self.

I release the need to compare myself to others.

I am proud of my accomplishments, big and small.

I trust in my ability to handle any challenge.

I am deserving of success and happiness.

I choose to see the good in myself and others.

47

I let go of negative self-talk and embrace positivity.

I honor my body and treat it with kindness and respect.
I am worthy of all the good things that come my way.

I forgive myself for past mistakes and learn from them.

I attract positive energy and people into my life.

I am confident in my ability to achieve my goals.

I am at peace with who I am becoming.

I deserve to prioritize self-care and self-love.

I am grateful for the unique person I am.

I trust my intuition to guide me in the right direction.
I am open to receiving compliments and praise.

I let go of fear and embrace courage.

I believe in my ability to create a life I love.

I am resilient and capable of overcoming any obstacle.

I see myself as valuable and worthy of love.

I am surrounded by people who uplift and support me.

I am worthy of all the opportunities that come my way.

I am confident in my ability to make positive choices.
I accept compliments graciously and believe in their truth.

I release the need for approval from others.

I am empowered to make choices that align with my values.

I acknowledge my worthiness of success and happiness.

I am proud of the person I am becoming.

I am comfortable being myself in all situations.

I am open to embracing new experiences and opportunities.

I trust in my ability to navigate life's challenges with grace.
I am confident in my ability to handle whatever comes my way.

I am worthy of love, kindness, and respect.

I see beauty in myself and in others.

I let go of self-doubt and embrace self-confidence.

I am worthy of pursuing my dreams and passions.

I am deserving of love and belonging.

I am comfortable setting boundaries that honor my well-being.

I am resilient and bounce back from setbacks with ease.
I am proud of my achievements and continue to strive for growth.

I am deserving of all the love, joy, and abundance life has to offer.

These affirmations can help foster positive, loving, and fulfilling relationships in your life when practiced regularly.

I am deserving of healthy and fulfilling relationships.

I attract loving and supportive people into my life.

I am open to giving and receiving love unconditionally.

I communicate with honesty, kindness, and compassion in my relationships.

I am worthy of respect and understanding from others.

I nurture my relationships with care and attention.
I am grateful for the connections I have with others.

I choose to forgive and let go of past hurts in my relationships.

I trust in the strength of my relationships to withstand challenges.

I am committed to creating harmony and balance in my relationships.

I am open to deepening my connections with others.

I honor and appreciate the differences in those I love.

I am worthy of love and belonging in all my relationships.
I choose to focus on the positive aspects of my relationships.

I am capable of resolving conflicts peacefully and constructively.

I cultivate empathy and understanding in my interactions with others.

I bring joy and positivity to my relationships.

I am deserving of genuine and authentic connections.

I prioritize quality time and meaningful conversations in my relationships.

I am worthy of being treated with kindness and respect.

I express my love and appreciation for others openly and sincerely.

I am surrounded by people who uplift and support me.

I trust in the process of building strong and lasting relationships.

I attract people who align with my values and aspirations.

I let go of toxic relationships and surround myself with positivity.

I am open to receiving love and support from those around me.

I communicate my needs and boundaries with clarity and confidence.
I am worthy of nurturing and fulfilling connections.

I choose to focus on building bridges rather than walls in my relationships.

I embrace vulnerability as a pathway to deeper intimacy.

I am grateful for the love and companionship I receive from others.

I am open to giving and receiving affection freely.

I release the need for approval from others and embrace self-love.

I am committed to investing time and effort into my relationships.
I honor the autonomy and individuality of those I love.

I attract healthy and balanced relationships into my life.

I am open to learning and growing from my relationships.

I trust in the divine timing of connections in my life.

I let go of expectations and accept others as they are.

I am deserving of loyalty and trust in my relationships.

I choose to focus on building mutual respect and understanding.

I am worthy of being loved deeply and completely.

I am surrounded by love and positivity in my relationships.

I am capable of creating a supportive and nurturing environment for my loved ones.

I trust in the power of love to heal and transform my relationships.

I am open to receiving guidance and support from those I love.

I am worthy of healthy boundaries that honor my well-being.

I choose to cultivate gratitude for the people who enrich my life.

I can foster strong and meaningful connections with others.

I am deserving of love, joy, and fulfillment in all my relationships.

These declarations reaffirm your commitment to honoring and respecting your spouse and family members by refraining from speaking negatively about them to others, thus nurturing trust and intimacy within your relationships.

I commit to always speaking positively and respectfully about my spouse and family members to others.

I refuse to engage in gossip or negative talk about my loved ones, recognizing the importance of preserving their dignity and honor.

I honor the sacred bond of marriage and family, and I vow to uphold it by speaking words of love and encouragement.

I choose to focus on the strengths and virtues of my spouse and family members, celebrating their uniqueness and individuality.

I recognize that speaking negatively about my loved ones only serves to harm our relationships and erode trust.

I value the trust and intimacy I share with my spouse and family, and I protect it by refraining from speaking ill of them behind their backs.

I embrace open and honest communication within my relationships, addressing concerns directly and respectfully.

I understand the power of words to shape perceptions and attitudes, and I use them to uplift and affirm my loved ones.

I refuse to participate in conversations that seek to tear down or criticize my spouse or family members.

I take responsibility for my own emotions and reactions, seeking constructive ways to address conflicts or disagreements within my relationships.

I cultivate a culture of love and respect within my family, where each member feels valued and appreciated.

I honor the sanctity of marriage and family by speaking words of love and affirmation, both in public and in private.

I cherish the bond I share with my spouse and family, and I protect it by speaking words of kindness and encouragement.

I recognize that every relationship has its challenges, but I am committed to addressing them with love and understanding.

I refuse to allow external influences to taint the sacredness of my relationships, and I guard them fiercely with my words and actions.
I prioritize the well-being and happiness of my loved ones, and I express this through my words and deeds.

I am grateful for the love and support of my spouse and family, and I honor them by speaking words of gratitude and appreciation.

I understand that speaking negatively about my loved ones only reflects poorly on myself, and I choose to uphold their honor and dignity at all times.

I foster an environment of trust and respect within my relationships, where communication is honest and authentic.

I commit to always speaking from a place of love and compassion, both in my words and in my actions towards my spouse and family.

These declarations reinforce your commitment to speaking up for yourself with courage and honesty, fostering authenticity and trust in all areas of your life.

I commit to speaking up for myself with courage and confidence, asserting my needs and boundaries in all areas of my life.

I refuse to silence my voice or suppress my truth, recognizing the importance of being transparent and honest with myself and others.

I embrace vulnerability as a strength, allowing myself to express my thoughts, feelings, and opinions openly and authentically.

I honor my values and integrity by speaking my truth with clarity and conviction, even when it may be difficult or uncomfortable.

I trust in my ability to communicate effectively and assertively, advocating for my interests and desires with grace and assertiveness.

I release the fear of judgment or rejection and embrace the freedom that comes from owning my truth and speaking it boldly.

I value honesty and transparency in all my relationships, fostering trust and authenticity through open communication.

I acknowledge my worth and deservingness of respect, and I refuse to settle for anything less than honest and transparent interactions.

I confront difficult situations with courage and resilience, addressing conflicts and misunderstandings with honesty and compassion.

I cultivate a culture of openness and authenticity in my workplace, business, and personal relationships, where transparency and honesty are valued and celebrated.

I embrace feedback as an opportunity for growth and self-improvement, welcoming constructive criticism with an open mind and a humble heart.

I communicate my boundaries clearly and assertively, respecting myself and others by upholding them consistently.

I honor my intuition and inner wisdom, trusting that speaking my truth will always lead me closer to alignment with my authentic self.

I refuse to compromise my values or integrity for the sake of conformity, choosing instead to stand firm in my truth and authenticity.

I speak from a place of compassion and empathy, recognizing the humanity in myself and others as I navigate difficult conversations with honesty and transparency.

I embrace the discomfort that comes from speaking up for myself, knowing that it is a necessary step towards personal growth and empowerment.

I release the need to please others at the expense of my own well-being, prioritizing my authenticity and self-respect above external validation.

I foster a culture of mutual respect and understanding in my relationships, where open and honest communication is encouraged and supported.

I take responsibility for my own happiness and fulfillment, advocating for my needs and desires with assertiveness and self-assurance.
I celebrate my courage and resilience in speaking up for myself, knowing that it is an act of self-love and empowerment that benefits both myself and those around me.

These declarations can empower you to establish and maintain healthy boundaries in your life, allowing you to prioritize your well-being and cultivate fulfilling relationships built on mutual respect and understanding.

I honor my needs and priorities by setting clear and healthy boundaries in all areas of my life.

I recognize that boundaries are essential for my well-being and I commit to establishing and maintaining them with compassion and assertiveness.

I trust myself to recognize when my boundaries are being tested and to take the necessary steps to enforce them with grace and integrity.

I release the guilt or fear of disappointing others when setting boundaries, knowing that my self-care is essential for living a fulfilling life.
I communicate my boundaries confidently and respectfully, understanding that doing so is an act of self-respect and self-love.

I surround myself with people who respect and honor my boundaries, and I distance myself from those who do not.

I trust that setting boundaries allows me to create space for positive and fulfilling relationships in my life.

I prioritize my mental, emotional, and physical well-being by establishing boundaries that protect my energy and preserve my peace of mind.

I am deserving of respect and consideration, and I enforce my boundaries with kindness and firmness.

I recognize that setting boundaries is an ongoing practice, and I commit to reassessing and adjusting them as needed to align with my evolving needs and values.

I take responsibility for enforcing my boundaries, knowing that doing so is an act of self-empowerment and self-care.

I release the need to justify or explain my boundaries to others, understanding that they are valid simply because they are mine.

I cultivate self-awareness and self-trust, allowing me to recognize when my boundaries are being crossed and to respond accordingly.

I create a safe and nurturing environment for myself by establishing boundaries that foster respect, understanding, and trust.

I communicate my boundaries with clarity and consistency, ensuring that others understand and respect them.

I prioritize my own needs and well-being without guilt or apology, knowing that self-care is essential for living a balanced and fulfilling life.

I recognize that setting boundaries is an act of self-love and self-respect, and I honor myself by enforcing them with courage and conviction.

I release the need to please others at the expense of my own well-being, and I prioritize myself by setting boundaries that honor my needs and values.

I trust that setting and enforcing boundaries will lead to deeper and more meaningful connections with others, based on mutual respect and understanding.
I celebrate my ability to set and enforce boundaries, knowing that doing so allows me to live authentically and in alignment with my true self.

These declarations can help you maintain your emotional well-being and protect your energy from toxic people, thoughts, and actions, allowing you to cultivate a life filled with positivity, joy, and fulfillment.

I choose to protect my energy by setting boundaries and distancing myself from toxic people and situations.

I refuse to engage with negativity or drama, knowing that my peace of mind is too valuable to sacrifice.

I release the need to fix or rescue others at the expense of my own well-being, prioritizing self-care, and self-preservation.

I trust my intuition to recognize toxic people and situations, and I have the courage to walk away from them with grace and dignity.
I cultivate a positive and empowering inner dialogue, banishing toxic thoughts and beliefs that do not serve my highest good.

I surround myself with people who uplift and inspire me, and I choose to invest my energy in relationships that nourish and support me.

I practice forgiveness and compassion towards those who may have hurt me, but I refuse to allow them to continue to drain my energy.

I set firm boundaries to protect myself from toxic behaviors and interactions, and I enforce them with confidence and assertiveness.

I release the need for approval or validation from toxic individuals, finding my worth and validation within myself.

I take responsibility for my own happiness and well-being, and I refuse to let toxic people or situations dim my light or dampen my spirit.

I cultivate resilience and inner strength, allowing me to rise above toxic influences and thrive in spite of them.

I focus on what I can control, letting go of the need to change or fix toxic people or situations that are beyond my control.

I practice self-care rituals that nourish my mind, body, and soul, replenishing my energy and protecting myself from the effects of toxicity.

I choose to respond with kindness and compassion to toxic behavior, knowing that it is often a reflection of someone else's pain or insecurity.

I release the need for conflict or confrontation with toxic individuals, opting instead to disengage and prioritize my own peace and well-being.

I trust in my ability to create a life free from toxicity, filled with love, joy, and abundance.

I cultivate gratitude for the lessons learned from toxic experiences, knowing that they have helped me grow stronger and wiser.

I surround myself with positivity and upliftment, filling my life with experiences and relationships that bring me joy and fulfillment.

I practice self-awareness and mindfulness, noticing when toxic influences begin to creep into my life and taking proactive steps to remove them.

I celebrate my ability to protect and preserve my energy, knowing that by doing so, I can live a life of peace, purpose, and fulfillment.

These declarations can empower you to take charge of your life and remove yourself from any negative situation with strength, confidence, and determination.

I am strong and resilient, capable of facing and overcoming any negative situation that comes my way.

I trust in my intuition and inner wisdom to guide me towards the right course of action in challenging circumstances.

I refuse to tolerate negativity or toxicity in my life, and I have the courage to remove myself from any situation that does not serve my highest good.

I release the fear of confrontation or conflict, knowing that my well-being is worth standing up for.
I embrace my power to create positive change in my life, starting by removing myself from negative environments or relationships.

I prioritize my mental, emotional, and physical well-being above all else, and I am willing to take decisive action to protect it.

I trust in my ability to handle whatever comes my way, knowing that I am capable and resourceful.

I refuse to be a victim of circumstances, and I take ownership of my life by removing myself from situations that no longer serve me.

I surround myself with supportive and uplifting influences, and I distance myself from anything or anyone that drains my energy or undermines my happiness.

I release the need for external validation or approval, finding strength and confidence from within myself.

I set firm boundaries to protect myself from negativity and toxicity, and I enforce them with courage and determination.

I refuse to allow fear to hold me back from taking action to improve my life, and I embrace the unknown with a sense of curiosity and adventure.

I trust that removing myself from negative situations will open up space for positive experiences and opportunities to flow into my life.

I acknowledge my worth and deservingness of happiness and fulfillment, and I refuse to settle for anything less. I cultivate resilience and adaptability, knowing that I have the strength to bounce back from any setback or challenge.

I release the need to explain or justify my decisions to others, knowing that my well-being is my highest priority.

I surround myself with people who uplift and support me, and I draw strength and inspiration from their positive energy.

I refuse to dwell on past mistakes or regrets, and I focus instead on creating a brighter future for myself.

I celebrate my courage and resilience in facing and removing myself from negative situations, knowing that each step forward brings me closer to a life of peace and fulfillment.

I am the architect of my own destiny, and I have the power to create a life filled with positivity, joy, and abundance.

These declarations can serve as affirmations to reinforce your commitment to breaking free from harmful habits and addictions, empowering you to take control of your life and create a future filled with health, happiness, and fulfillment.

I release the grip of addiction and reclaim control over my life and my choices.

I am worthy of a life free from destructive habits, and I have the strength to overcome them.

I let go of the need for external validation and find fulfillment within myself.

I am capable of breaking free from the hold of addiction and creating a life of purpose and meaning.

I choose to prioritize my well-being over temporary indulgences that hinder my growth and happiness.

I release the power that addiction holds over me and embrace the freedom that comes with breaking free.

I am committed to my journey of recovery and healing, knowing that each step forward brings me closer to wholeness.

I replace destructive habits with healthy coping mechanisms that nurture my mind, body, and soul.

I forgive myself for past mistakes and focus on the present moment, where I have the power to make positive changes.

*I surround myself with supportive and understanding individuals who uplift and encourage me on my journey.
I am resilient in the face of temptation and refuse to let setbacks derail my progress towards recovery.*

I trust in my ability to overcome challenges and emerge stronger and more empowered on the other side.

I let go of shame and guilt associated with my past behaviors and embrace a future filled with hope and possibility.

I acknowledge the impact of my habits on my mental, emotional, and physical well-being, and I commit to making positive changes.

I take ownership of my actions and choices, knowing that I have the power to shape my destiny.

*I am deserving of a life free from the chains of addiction, and I am willing to do whatever it takes to break them.
I am grateful for the opportunity to embark on a journey of self-discovery and transformation.*

I release the need for instant gratification and embrace the process of long-term growth and fulfillment.

I cultivate self-awareness and mindfulness, allowing me to recognize triggers and patterns that contribute to addictive behaviors.

I celebrate my progress and victories, no matter how small, and remain steadfast in my commitment to living a life of freedom and authenticity.

These declarations can help you shift your mindset and habits away from heavy social media usage, allowing you to reclaim control of your time, energy, and focus for more fulfilling pursuits.

I reclaim my time and energy from excessive social media usage.

I prioritize real-life connections and experiences over virtual interactions.

I set boundaries for myself regarding social media usage and stick to them with determination.

I recognize the negative impact of heavy social media use on my mental and emotional well-being.

I limit my social media usage to specific times of the day, allowing myself to focus on other important aspects of my life.
I find fulfillment and joy in activities that don't involve social media, such as spending time outdoors, pursuing hobbies, or connecting with loved ones.

I cultivate mindfulness and presence in the moment, rather than getting lost in the endless scroll of social media feeds.

I take regular breaks from social media to recharge and rejuvenate my mind and spirit.

I delete or unfollow accounts that trigger negative emotions or comparisons, creating a more positive and uplifting social media environment.

I practice gratitude for the present moment, recognizing that life's true beauty lies beyond the confines of a screen.

I resist the urge to mindlessly scroll through social media and instead engage in activities that nurture my growth and well-being.

I prioritize self-care and self-love, recognizing that my worth is not determined by likes, comments, or followers.

I cultivate meaningful connections with others outside of social media, fostering deeper and more authentic relationships.

I acknowledge that social media is just one aspect of my life and not the sole source of validation or fulfillment.

I focus on living my life to the fullest, rather than curating it for the approval of others on social media.

I set specific goals and intentions for my time spent on social media, ensuring that it aligns with my values and priorities.

I practice moderation and balance in my social media usage, recognizing when it's time to log off and engage in activities that bring me joy and fulfillment.

I embrace boredom as an opportunity for creativity and self-reflection, rather than turning to social media for constant stimulation.

I seek out alternative sources of entertainment and information, diversifying my experiences beyond the confines of social media.

I celebrate my progress in reducing my social media usage and acknowledge the positive impact it has on my overall well-being.

These declarations can help shift your mindset and behavior away from gossip and negative talk, fostering a culture of kindness, respect, and positivity in your relationships and interactions with others.

I choose to speak with kindness and compassion, refraining from gossip and negative talk about others.

I recognize the harmful impact of gossip and negative speech, and I commit to breaking this cycle.

I cultivate empathy and understanding towards others, refraining from passing judgment or spreading rumors.

I honor the dignity and humanity of every individual, refusing to engage in conversations that undermine their character or reputation.

I focus on uplifting and empowering others through my words and actions, rather than tearing them down.

I take responsibility for the energy I bring into conversations, ensuring that it is positive and uplifting.

I practice active listening and open-mindedness, seeking to understand others without jumping to conclusions or making assumptions.

I set a positive example for others by choosing to speak with words of encouragement and support.

I refrain from participating in gossip or negative talk, even when tempted to do so by others.

I recognize that gossiping reflects poorly on my own character and integrity, and I choose to rise above it.
I redirect conversations away from gossip and negativity towards topics that are uplifting and meaningful.

I speak up against gossip and negative talk when I encounter it, advocating for kindness and respect in all interactions.

I release the need to compare myself to others or tear them down in order to feel better about myself.

I focus on my own growth and self-improvement, rather than getting caught up in the shortcomings of others.

I practice forgiveness and compassion towards those who may have wronged me, refusing to hold onto resentment or bitterness.

I surround myself with positive influences and engage in conversations that uplift and inspire me.
I take a moment to pause and reflect before speaking, ensuring that my words align with my values and intentions.

I choose to see the best in others and assume positive intentions, rather than jumping to negative conclusions.

I seek out opportunities to build others up and celebrate their successes, rather than tearing them down out of jealousy or insecurity.

I commit to creating a culture of kindness and respect in my relationships and interactions with others.

STOP BLAMING OTHERS, TAKE ACCOUNTABILITY.

These declarations can help you cultivate a mindset of self-accountability and empowerment, empowering you to take ownership of your life and make positive changes that lead to personal growth and success.

I take full responsibility for my life and my choices, recognizing that I alone have the power to create the life I desire.

I release the need to blame others for my circumstances and instead focus on what I can do to improve them.

I embrace accountability for my actions and their consequences, knowing that I am the architect of my own destiny.

I refuse to make excuses for why I can't achieve my goals, and instead, I focus on finding solutions and taking action.

I let go of the victim mentality and step into my power as the creator of my own reality.

I acknowledge that challenges and setbacks are opportunities for growth and learning, not excuses for failure.

I take ownership of my mistakes and use them as stepping stones towards personal development and success.

I refuse to dwell on past failures or mistakes, choosing instead to focus on the present moment and the possibilities it holds.

I am committed to continuous growth and improvement, and I refuse to let fear or excuses hold me back from reaching my full potential.
I replace blame with self-reflection and introspection, seeking to understand how I can become a better version of myself.

I let go of the need for external validation and approval, finding validation within myself and my own sense of worth.

I cultivate a mindset of possibility and abundance, knowing that there are always opportunities for growth and success.

I surround myself with positive influences and support systems that uplift and encourage me on my journey.

I embrace discomfort as a catalyst for growth, knowing that true transformation happens outside of my comfort zone.

I refuse to make excuses for why I can't achieve my dreams, and instead, I take bold and decisive action towards making them a reality.

I accept that I may face obstacles and challenges along the way, but I am confident in my ability to overcome them with resilience and determination.

I let go of limiting beliefs that hold me back from reaching my full potential, replacing them with empowering thoughts and beliefs.

I am the master of my fate and the captain of my soul, and I refuse to let anything stand in the way of my success.

I embrace the journey of self-discovery and personal growth, knowing that each step forward brings me closer to becoming the best version of myself.

I am worthy of success, happiness, and fulfillment, and I refuse to settle for anything less than the life I truly desire.

YOU ALWAYS HAVE A CHOICE! YOUR CHOICES DIRECTLY REFLECT YOUR RESULTS.

These declarations reinforce your agency and responsibility in shaping your life's outcomes while highlighting the importance of making empowered choices aligned with your goals and values.

I am the creator of my own destiny, and I take full responsibility for the results I achieve in life.

I refuse to blame external circumstances for my outcomes, knowing that I always have a choice in the actions I take.

I am empowered to shape my reality through my thoughts, words, and actions, and I embrace this power with gratitude and determination.

I release the need for validation or approval from others and trust in my ability to create the life I desire.

I acknowledge that my choices determine my destiny, and I am committed to making choices that align with my values and goals.

I am the captain of my ship, navigating through life with purpose, intention, and integrity.

I embrace the principle of cause and effect, understanding that every action I take has a corresponding result.

I take ownership of my decisions and their outcomes, using them as opportunities for growth and self-improvement.

I refuse to be a victim of circumstances, and instead, I choose to be the architect of my own success.
I trust in my ability to make wise and empowered choices that lead to positive outcomes in all areas of my life.

I am accountable for my own happiness and fulfillment, and I refuse to delegate this responsibility to anyone else.

I release the need for external validation and approval, finding validation within myself and my own sense of worth.

I embrace the power of choice as a gift that allows me to create the life of my dreams.

I am committed to living a life of purpose and intention, guided by the choices I make each day.

I take full ownership of my successes and failures, knowing that they are a reflection of the choices I have made.
I refuse to be limited by fear or self-doubt, and instead, I choose to step into my power and take decisive action towards my goals.

I trust in my intuition and inner wisdom to guide me towards the right choices and actions for my highest good.

I am the author of my own story, and I write each chapter with intention, courage, and authenticity.

I embrace the journey of self-discovery and personal growth, knowing that every choice I make brings me closer to my truest self.

I am empowered to create the life of my dreams, and I am committed to making choices that align with my vision and values.

These affirmations provide a strong foundation for cultivating a positive mindset to eliminate debt.

I am releasing myself from the burden of debt.

Financial freedom is my birthright, and I claim it now.

I attract abundance and prosperity into my life.

I am in control of my finances, and I manage them wisely.

Every day, I move closer to a debt-free life.

I am capable of overcoming any financial challenge that comes my way.

I release any fear or anxiety about money and welcome abundance.
My bank account is growing, and my debts are shrinking.

I am grateful for the lessons learned from my past financial struggles.

I am aligning my actions with my financial goals.

I attract opportunities to increase my income and eliminate debt.

I trust in my ability to create a stable and prosperous financial future.

I release any attachment to material possessions and focus on financial freedom.

I am breaking free from the cycle of debt and building wealth.
I am worthy of a life free from financial stress and worry.

I make smart financial decisions that lead me to a debt-free life.

I am attracting financial abundance with every positive thought.

I let go of the past and embrace a future filled with financial freedom.

I am committed to living within my means and achieving financial stability.

I am grateful for the resources and support available to help me eliminate debt.

I release any guilt or shame associated with past financial mistakes.
I trust that the universe provides me with everything I need to become debt-free.

I am creating a life of abundance and prosperity for myself and my loved ones.

I am confident in my ability to achieve my financial goals and live debt-free.

I deserve to live a life free from the burden of debt.
I am open to receiving guidance and support on my journey to financial freedom.

I trust that I am always provided for, and I release any scarcity mindset.

I am capable of creating a life of abundance and prosperity for myself and others.

I am open to receiving unexpected blessings and abundance in my life.

I am worthy of experiencing financial abundance and prosperity.

These affirmations can be recited daily to cultivate a positive mindset and support the achievement of health and fitness goals.

I am committed to nourishing my body with wholesome foods.

I prioritize my health and well-being every day.

I am grateful for the opportunity to improve my health through fitness and nutrition.

I choose to fuel my body with foods that promote vitality and energy.

I honor my body by engaging in regular exercise and movement.

Each day, I move closer to achieving my fitness goals.
I trust in my body's ability to heal and thrive with proper care.

I release any negative thoughts about my body and embrace self-love and acceptance.

I am dedicated to making positive choices that support my health and vitality.

I am worthy of investing time and effort into my physical well-being.

I celebrate my progress and accomplishments on my health journey.

I let go of unhealthy habits and embrace a lifestyle that promotes vitality.

I am in tune with my body's needs and respond to them with love and care.
I choose to view exercise and healthy eating as acts of self-love and self-respect.

I am grateful for the strength and resilience of my body.

I trust the process of transformation and honor the journey towards optimal health.

I am capable of achieving my fitness goals through consistent effort and dedication.

I release any fear or doubt about my ability to create positive changes in my health.

I am open to trying new activities and foods that benefit my overall well-being.

I listen to my body's signals and give it the rest and nourishment it needs.
I am grateful for the opportunity to cultivate a healthy and vibrant life.

I choose to focus on progress, not perfection, on my health journey.

I am deserving of a body that is strong, vibrant, and full of vitality.

I am committed to making sustainable lifestyle changes that support my health goals.

I am empowered to take control of my health and create positive habits.

I trust in my body's innate wisdom to guide me towards optimal health.

I am grateful for the abundance of nutritious foods that nourish my body.
I embrace the journey of self-discovery and growth on my path to wellness.

I release any negative beliefs about my body and replace them with love and gratitude.

I am worthy of investing in activities and practices that promote my physical and mental well-being.

I choose to view exercise as an opportunity to strengthen and empower myself.

I am grateful for the opportunity to prioritize my health and well-being.

I release any attachment to unhealthy habits and embrace a lifestyle of balance and moderation.

I trust that each step I take towards better health brings me closer to my goals.
I am open to receiving support and guidance on my journey to improved health.

I am grateful for the progress I've made and excited for the transformations yet to come.

I am worthy of experiencing vibrant health and vitality.

I choose to view food as nourishment for my body and fuel for my life.

I am committed to creating a healthy and balanced lifestyle that supports my well-being.

I am grateful for the opportunity to care for my body and prioritize my health.

These affirmations can help reinforce the mindset of not taking things personally, fostering inner peace, self-assurance, and emotional resilience.

I release the need to take things personally and remain grounded in my truth.

I recognize that the actions and words of others are a reflection of their own experiences and perceptions.

I choose to detach emotionally from situations that may trigger feelings of personal offense.

I honor my boundaries and refuse to internalize negativity directed towards me.

I cultivate a mindset of resilience and self-assurance, knowing that my worth is not defined by others' opinions or actions.
I practice compassion towards myself and others, understanding that everyone is navigating their own journey.

I release the burden of trying to please everyone and focus on living authentically.

I trust in my own perspective and intuition, allowing me to navigate interactions with clarity and grace.

I affirm my worthiness and value, independent of external validation or criticism.

I embrace the power of forgiveness, both towards myself and those who may unintentionally cause hurt.

I choose to respond to challenging situations with empathy and understanding rather than defensiveness.
I acknowledge that misunderstandings may arise but remain confident in my ability to communicate effectively.

I release the need to control others' perceptions of me and instead focus on cultivating inner peace.

I affirm my right to prioritize my well-being and mental health above the opinions of others.

I practice mindfulness, staying present in the moment and avoiding the trap of overthinking.

I am resilient in the face of criticism or rejection, recognizing that they are opportunities for growth and self-reflection.

I choose to focus on the positive aspects of myself and my life rather than dwelling on perceived shortcomings.
I affirm my inherent worthiness and refuse to allow external circumstances to diminish it.

I trust in my ability to handle difficult situations with grace and dignity, knowing that I am capable of resilience.

I release the need for validation from others and find solace in my own sense of self-worth.

I affirm my right to set healthy boundaries and protect my emotional well-being.

I recognize that everyone is entitled to their own opinions and perspectives, and I respect their right to express them.

I release the need to internalize criticism or negativity from others, knowing that it says more about them than it does about me.

I choose to respond to challenging situations with love and understanding, rather than allowing them to trigger feelings of defensiveness.

I affirm my right to prioritize my own needs and well-being, even if it means disappointing others.

I release the need to seek approval or validation from others and instead find validation within myself.

I trust in my own judgment and intuition, knowing that I am capable of making wise decisions for myself.

I affirm my right to speak my truth and express myself authentically, regardless of others' reactions.

I choose to focus on the positive aspects of myself and my life, rather than dwelling on perceived shortcomings or failures.

I release the need to compare myself to others and instead celebrate my own unique qualities and accomplishments.

These affirmations can serve as a daily reminder to deepen your relationship with God (if you believe in the divine), nurture your spirituality, and cultivate conscientiousness in all aspects of your life. True self improvement comes from mind, body, and soul. Feeding the soul is very important, however your beliefs are.

I am deeply connected to the divine presence within and around me.

I trust in the guidance and wisdom of the universe to lead me on my spiritual path.

Each day, I grow closer to God and feel His love and guidance in my life.

I am open to receiving divine inspiration and insights that align with my highest good.

I surrender my worries and fears to God, knowing that He will guide me through any challenge.

I am a vessel of love and light, sharing compassion and kindness with all beings.

I honor the sacredness of all life and treat every living being with respect and reverence.

I am attuned to the whispers of my soul and follow its guidance with trust and faith.

I embrace the journey of self-discovery and spiritual growth with courage and humility.

I cultivate a deep sense of gratitude for the blessings and miracles in my life.

I am a channel of divine grace, allowing love and healing to flow through me.
I trust in the divine timing of all things and surrender to the unfolding of my soul's journey.

I am worthy of experiencing profound peace, joy, and abundance in my life.

I nourish my spirit with prayer, meditation, and acts of service to others.

I align my thoughts, words, and actions with the highest truth and integrity.

I am a beacon of light, shining God's love and compassion into the world.

I seek to understand and embrace the interconnectedness of all creation.

I honor my unique gifts and talents, knowing that they are divine expressions of God's love.

I release any attachments to material possessions and embrace a life of simplicity and gratitude.

I am guided by the divine wisdom within me to make choices that align with my soul's purpose.

I surrender to the divine plan for my life, trusting that it is perfect and for my highest good.

I am filled with faith and confidence in God's infinite love and abundance.

I am a co-creator with God, manifesting love, peace, and harmony in my life and in the world.

I forgive myself and others, knowing that forgiveness is a sacred act that heals and frees the soul.

I am open to receiving divine guidance and inspiration in every moment of my life.

I cultivate a heart of compassion and empathy, seeing the divine spark in all beings.

I am a conduit for divine healing energy, bringing comfort and solace to those in need.

I trust in the power of prayer to uplift and transform my life and the lives of others.

I surrender my ego to the divine will, allowing God's wisdom and grace to guide me.

I am a divine being, worthy of love, joy, and abundance in all areas of my life.

I honor the sacredness of my body, mind, and spirit, caring for them with love and respect.
I am connected to the infinite wisdom and love of the universe, and I am always supported and guided.

I surrender to the divine flow of life, knowing that everything happens for a reason and serves my highest good.

I am grateful for the blessings of each day, knowing that they are gifts from God.

I trust in the divine plan for my life and have faith that everything is unfolding perfectly.

I am a co-creator with God, and together we bring love, light, and healing to the world.

I release any fear or doubt and trust in the divine protection and guidance that surrounds me.

I am a divine being of light and love, and I am here to shine my radiance into the world.

I am aligned with the divine purpose of my soul, and I follow its guidance with courage and trust.

I am grateful for the divine presence that fills me with peace, joy, and love each day.

These affirmations can help cultivate a mindset of generosity, kindness, and compassion, inspiring you to make a positive difference in the lives of others every day. All the things you may want for yourself are best received when you give them to someone else. The Universe has a way of rewarding those beyond your desires when you bless others.

I find joy in serving and uplifting others.

My purpose is to make a positive difference in the lives of those around me.

I am grateful for the opportunity to contribute to the well-being of others.

Compassion and kindness flow effortlessly from my heart.

I prioritize the needs of others with love and generosity. Each day, I seek out opportunities to offer support and assistance to those in need.

I am a beacon of light, bringing hope and encouragement to those who are struggling.

I am committed to acts of kindness and service as a way of life.

I am grateful for the abundance in my life, and I share it generously with others.

I am attentive to the needs of those around me and offer my help willingly.

I am a source of strength and support for my friends, family, and community.

I give freely of my time, talents, and resources to make a positive impact in the world.
I recognize the inherent worth and dignity of every person, and I treat them with respect and compassion.

I am a catalyst for positive change, inspiring others to acts of kindness and generosity.

I am deeply fulfilled by the joy and gratitude of those I am able to help.

I am grateful for the privilege of being able to give back to others.

I approach each interaction with empathy, seeking to understand and alleviate the suffering of others.

I am a force for good in the world, spreading love and compassion wherever I go.

I am blessed with abundance so that I may share it generously with others.

I am grateful for the opportunity to make a positive impact in the lives of others.

I am attuned to the needs of those around me, and I offer my support willingly and compassionately.

I am committed to making a difference in the world, one act of kindness at a time.

I am grateful for the ability to bring comfort and solace to those who are hurting.

I am a conduit for divine love and compassion, sharing it freely with all those I encounter.

I am deeply fulfilled by the connections I make and the lives I am able to touch through my acts of kindness.

I am grateful for the opportunity to serve others and make a positive impact in the world.

I am blessed with abundance so that I may share it generously with those in need.

I approach each interaction with an open heart and a willingness to help others in any way I can.

I am a source of strength and support for those who are struggling, offering my love and compassion unconditionally.

I am committed to making the world a better place by giving freely of my time, talents, and resources.

I am grateful for the opportunity to be of service to others and make a meaningful difference in their lives.
I am attuned to the needs of those around me and offer my support with kindness and compassion.

I am a beacon of hope and inspiration, uplifting others with my acts of kindness and generosity.

I am deeply fulfilled by the impact I am able to make in the lives of others through my acts of service.

I am grateful for the abundance in my life and share it generously with those in need.

I approach each day with a spirit of generosity and compassion, seeking out opportunities to help others.

I am blessed with the resources to make a positive impact in the world, and I use them wisely and compassionately.
I am deeply fulfilled by the connections I make and the lives I am able to touch through my acts of kindness and generosity.

I am grateful for the opportunity to give back to others and make a meaningful difference in their lives.

I am a source of love and light, spreading joy and compassion wherever I go.

These affirmations can help professional athletes cultivate a mindset of confidence, focus, and determination, empowering them to perform at their best in every practice and competition.

I am a dedicated and disciplined athlete, committed to reaching my full potential.

I trust in my training and preparation to excel in my sport.

I am focused and fully present in every practice and competition.

I believe in my abilities to perform at the highest level.

I am mentally tough and resilient, capable of overcoming any challenge.

I embrace pressure and use it as fuel to drive my performance.

I am in peak physical condition, ready to compete with strength and agility.

I visualize success and victory in every aspect of my sport.

I am confident in my skills and talents, knowing that I am capable of greatness.

I approach every opportunity to compete with a winning mindset.

I am relentless in my pursuit of excellence, always striving to improve.

I am a champion, and I compete with the heart of a winner. I am fearless in the face of adversity, rising to the occasion with courage and determination.

I trust my instincts and intuition to guide me to victory.

I am disciplined in my preparation, knowing that hard work always pays off.

I am focused on my goals and committed to achieving them through dedication and perseverance.

I am resilient in the face of setbacks, bouncing back stronger and more determined than ever.

I am disciplined in my approach to training, nutrition, and recovery, ensuring peak performance.

I am a master of my craft, constantly honing my skills and refining my technique.
I am driven by passion and purpose, fueled by the desire to be the best.

I am mentally and emotionally prepared to compete at my best.

I am confident in my ability to rise to the occasion and deliver when it matters most.

I am focused on the present moment, letting go of distractions and staying in the zone.

I am surrounded by a supportive team that believes in me and helps me succeed.

I am grateful for the opportunity to compete and showcase my talents.

I am committed to giving my all in every practice, knowing that it prepares me for success.
I am a student of the game, always learning and growing to stay ahead of the competition.

I am driven by a relentless pursuit of greatness, never settling for anything less than my best.

I am mentally tough and unshakeable, able to perform under pressure with calm confidence.

I am a fierce competitor, hungry for victory and willing to do whatever it takes to win.

I am focused on the process, trusting that results will come with consistent effort and dedication.

I am grateful for the opportunity to compete against the best, knowing that it pushes me to be better.
I am disciplined in my habits and routines, knowing that they lay the foundation for success.

I am a champion in the making, destined for greatness through hard work and determination.

I am driven by passion and purpose, fueling my desire to succeed at the highest level.

I am mentally and physically prepared to perform at my best, no matter the circumstances.

I am confident in my abilities and trust that I have what it takes to succeed.

I am relentless in my pursuit of excellence, pushing myself to new heights with every challenge.
I am focused on my goals and committed to achieving them through relentless effort and determination.

I am grateful for the opportunity to compete and showcase my talents on the world stage.

These affirmations can help professionals in the corporate world cultivate a mindset of confidence, resilience, and success, empowering them to thrive in their careers and make a positive impact in their organizations.

I am a skilled and capable professional, fully equipped to navigate the challenges of the corporate world.

I approach each day with confidence, knowing that I have the knowledge and expertise to succeed.

I am committed to excellence in all aspects of my work, striving for continuous improvement.

I am an asset to my team and contribute valuable insights and ideas to our collective success.

I embrace challenges as opportunities for growth and learning.

I am focused and productive, maximizing my efficiency and effectiveness in everything I do.
I am a confident and persuasive communicator, able to convey my ideas with clarity and conviction.

I am resilient in the face of setbacks, adapting and persevering until I achieve my goals.

I am proactive and resourceful, always seeking out new opportunities to add value and make a difference.

I am a leader in my field, respected for my integrity, professionalism, and expertise.

I am grateful for the opportunities I have to learn, grow, and contribute in the corporate world.
I am open to feedback and constructive criticism, using it as fuel for my personal and professional development.

I am committed to building positive and collaborative relationships with my colleagues and clients.

I am dedicated to delivering results that exceed expectations and drive the success of my organization.

I am adaptable and flexible, able to thrive in a fast-paced and ever-changing business environment.

I am driven by a sense of purpose and passion for my work, fueling my determination to succeed.

I am confident in my ability to overcome any obstacles that stand in the way of my success.
I am a strategic thinker, able to anticipate challenges and develop innovative solutions.

I am disciplined in my approach to work, managing my time and priorities effectively.

I am committed to maintaining a healthy work-life balance, prioritizing my well-being and happiness.

I am grateful for the support and mentorship I receive from my colleagues and leaders.

I am constantly expanding my knowledge and skills to stay ahead in the competitive corporate world.

I am focused on results, consistently achieving my targets and exceeding expectations.

I am a leader who leads by example, inspiring others with my dedication and work ethic.

I am grateful for the opportunities I have to make a meaningful impact in the corporate world.

I am a problem solver, able to find creative solutions to complex challenges.

I am a team player, collaborating with others to achieve our shared goals and objectives.

I am disciplined in my habits and routines, ensuring consistency and reliability in my work.

I am respected for my professionalism, integrity, and commitment to excellence.

I am grateful for the growth and development opportunities available to me in the corporate world.

I am focused on continuous improvement, always striving to raise the bar and achieve new heights.

I am confident in my ability to navigate the complexities of the corporate world with grace and ease.

I am a visionary leader, inspiring others with my passion, vision, and determination.

I am dedicated to creating a positive and inclusive work environment where everyone can thrive.

I am grateful for the support and encouragement I receive from my colleagues and peers.
I am a problem solver, able to approach challenges with creativity and ingenuity.

I am committed to fostering a culture of innovation and collaboration in my organization.

I am resilient in the face of adversity, bouncing back stronger and more determined than ever.

I am grateful for the opportunities I have to learn and grow in the corporate world.

I am a visionary leader, inspiring others to embrace change and pursue excellence.

These affirmations can help entrepreneurs and business owners cultivate a mindset of focus, determination, and success, empowering them to achieve their goals and make a lasting impact in their industries.

I am the architect of my destiny, and I create success with every decision I make.

I am committed to achieving my goals and turning my dreams into reality.

I take full responsibility for my actions and hold myself accountable for my success.

I am focused and determined, channeling my energy into activities that move me closer to my goals.

I am driven by a burning desire to succeed, and I will not let anything stand in my way.
I am disciplined in my habits and routines, maximizing my productivity and efficiency.

I am a visionary leader, inspiring others with my passion and determination.

I am resilient in the face of adversity, bouncing back stronger and more determined than ever.

I am grateful for the opportunities I have to learn and grow as an entrepreneur.

I am committed to pushing past my comfort zone and embracing new challenges.

I am a problem solver, approaching obstacles with creativity and ingenuity.

I am constantly expanding my knowledge and skills to stay ahead in the competitive business world.
I am focused on results, consistently achieving my targets and exceeding expectations.

I am grateful for the support and encouragement I receive from my team and mentors.

I am a master of my craft, constantly honing my skills and refining my strategies.

I am adaptable and flexible, able to pivot and adjust course when necessary.

I am confident in my ability to navigate the complexities of entrepreneurship with grace and ease.

I am a beacon of inspiration and innovation, leading by example and empowering others to succeed.

I am committed to creating a positive and inclusive work environment where everyone can thrive.

I am driven by a sense of purpose and passion for my work, fueling my determination to succeed.

I am focused on the present moment, letting go of distractions and staying laser-focused on my goals.

I am grateful for the growth and development opportunities available to me as an entrepreneur.

I am a strategic thinker, able to anticipate challenges and develop innovative solutions.

I am disciplined in my approach to work, managing my time and priorities effectively.
I am a visionary leader, inspiring others with my vision, integrity, and commitment to excellence.

I am grateful for the freedom and flexibility that comes with being an entrepreneur.

I am open to new ideas and opportunities, always seeking ways to innovate and improve.

I am a relentless optimist, seeing challenges as opportunities for growth and learning.

I am a lifelong learner, committed to continuous improvement and personal development.

I am grateful for the opportunity to make a positive impact in the world through my business.

I am focused on building a legacy of success that will inspire future generations.

I am a magnet for abundance and prosperity, attracting wealth and success into my life.

I am committed to serving others and making a meaningful difference in their lives.

I am grateful for the freedom and flexibility that comes with owning my own business.

I am a visionary leader, able to see the big picture and inspire others to join me on the journey.

I am disciplined in my pursuit of success, willing to do whatever it takes to achieve my goals.

I am committed to building a business that reflects my values and makes a positive impact in the world.

I am grateful for the opportunities I have to learn and grow as an entrepreneur.

I am focused on the future, always looking for ways to innovate and stay ahead of the curve.

I am driven by a deep sense of purpose and passion, fueling my determination to succeed.

These affirmations can help reinforce the mindset of acting towards one's dreams, fostering determination, resilience, and gratitude along the journey of manifestation.

My dreams are within reach, and I am taking decisive action to bring them to fruition.

I am the architect of my destiny, and I am actively creating the life of my dreams.

I am committed to pursuing my dreams with unwavering determination and perseverance.

I am courageous and bold, fearlessly stepping outside of my comfort zone to chase my dreams.

I trust in my abilities and believe in my potential to achieve greatness.
Each day, I move closer to my dreams by taking intentional and inspired actions.

I am aligned with my purpose, and I am fully committed to realizing my deepest aspirations.

I embrace challenges as opportunities for growth and learning on my journey towards my dreams.

I am focused and disciplined, channeling my energy into actions that propel me towards my goals.

I am driven by passion and purpose, fueling my determination to make my dreams a reality.

I am worthy of living a life filled with abundance, joy, and fulfillment.
I am grateful for the opportunities that come my way, and I seize them with enthusiasm and gratitude.

I am confident in my ability to overcome obstacles and persevere through setbacks on my path to success.

I am constantly expanding my knowledge and skills to become the best version of myself.

I am surrounded by love and support as I pursue my dreams, and I am deeply grateful for the encouragement of those around me.

I am a magnet for success, attracting opportunities and resources that help me achieve my goals.

I am persistent and resilient, never giving up on my dreams even in the face of adversity.
I am the master of my fate and the captain of my soul, charting my course towards my dreams with courage and determination.

I am grateful for the journey towards my dreams, embracing every experience as a stepping stone to my ultimate destination.

I am living my dreams each day, knowing that every action I take brings me closer to my desired reality.

I am focused on the present moment, fully immersed in the journey of manifesting my dreams.

I am committed to taking consistent and purposeful action towards my goals, knowing that each step forward brings me closer to my dreams.

I am aligned with the universe, and I trust in its divine guidance to lead me towards the fulfillment of my dreams.

I am a co-creator of my reality, and I am manifesting my dreams with intention, clarity, and purpose.

I am grateful for the courage and determination within me that propels me forward on the path to my dreams.

I am unstoppable in my pursuit of my dreams, and I am willing to do whatever it takes to make them a reality.

I am committed to stepping out of my comfort zone and embracing new challenges that bring me closer to my dreams.

I am empowered to turn my dreams into reality, and I trust in my ability to overcome any obstacles that may arise.
I am deserving of all the success and abundance that comes my way as I follow my dreams with passion and determination.

I am grateful for the clarity of vision that guides me towards my dreams, and I trust in the process of manifestation to bring them to fruition.

I am living my dreams each day, and I am deeply grateful for the abundance and blessings that flow into my life as a result.

I am committed to taking inspired action towards my dreams, knowing that every step I take brings me closer to my desired reality.

I am a powerful creator, and I am manifesting my dreams with intention, purpose, and unwavering faith.

I am aligned with the universe, and I trust in its divine plan for me as I journey towards the fulfillment of my dreams.

I am grateful for the resilience and perseverance within me that allows me to overcome any challenges that stand in the way of my dreams.

I am worthy of all the success and abundance that comes my way as I follow my dreams with courage and determination. I am unstoppable in my pursuit of my dreams, and I am willing to take bold and decisive action to make them a reality.

I am empowered to create the life of my dreams, and I trust in my ability to turn my visions into tangible manifestations.

I am committed to following my heart and intuition as I navigate the journey towards my dreams, knowing that they will always lead me in the right direction.

I am living my dreams each day, and I am deeply grateful for the sense of purpose, fulfillment, and joy that they bring into my life.

These affirmations can help reinforce a mindset of abundance, wealth, and prosperity, aligning your thoughts and actions with the goal of becoming a multi-millionaire.

I am worthy of abundance and success beyond my wildest dreams.

I attract wealth and prosperity into my life with ease and grace.

I am a magnet for financial abundance and opportunities.

I believe in my ability to create wealth and abundance in all areas of my life.

I am open to receiving limitless abundance from expected and unexpected sources.

I am aligned with the energy of abundance, and it flows freely into my life.

I am grateful for the abundance that surrounds me and for the abundance that is on its way.

I release any limiting beliefs about money and embrace my unlimited potential to amass wealth.

I am deserving of all the riches and success that the universe has in store for me.

I am financially savvy and make smart decisions that lead to wealth accumulation.

I am confident in my ability to manage and grow my wealth wisely.

I am committed to taking bold actions that lead to financial abundance and prosperity.
I am surrounded by a supportive network of mentors, advisors, and allies who help me achieve my financial goals.

I am grateful for the opportunities that come my way and seize them with confidence and enthusiasm.

I am a master of my finances and take full responsibility for my financial well-being.

I am worthy of experiencing the lifestyle of my dreams, filled with luxury, freedom, and joy.

I am aligned with the energy of wealth and abundance, and it flows effortlessly into my life.

I am open to receiving and giving generously, knowing that the more I give, the more I receive.

I am a powerful creator, and I manifest my desires with clarity, focus, and intention.

I am grateful for the abundance that I have already manifested and excited for the even greater abundance that is on its way.

I am financially independent and free to live life on my own terms.

I am worthy of receiving wealth and abundance in all areas of my life.

I am open to new ideas and opportunities that lead to financial abundance and success.

I am committed to my financial goals and take consistent action towards achieving them.

I am aligned with the energy of prosperity and success, and it flows effortlessly into my life.
I am a conscious steward of wealth, using my resources to create positive change in the world.

I am grateful for the abundance that I have already manifested and excited for the even greater abundance that is on its way.

I am worthy of receiving wealth and abundance in all areas of my life.

I am open to new ideas and opportunities that lead to financial abundance and success.

I am committed to my financial goals and take consistent action towards achieving them.

I am aligned with the energy of prosperity and success, and it flows effortlessly into my life.

I am a conscious steward of wealth, using my resources to create positive change in the world.

I am grateful for the abundance that I have already manifested and excited for the even greater abundance that is on its way.

I am worthy of receiving wealth and abundance in all areas of my life.

I am open to new ideas and opportunities that lead to financial abundance and success.

I am committed to my financial goals and take consistent action towards achieving them.

I am aligned with the energy of prosperity and success, and it flows effortlessly into my life.

I am a conscious steward of wealth, using my resources to create positive change in the world.

I am grateful for the abundance that I have already manifested and excited for the even greater abundance that is on its way.

I am worthy of receiving wealth and abundance in all areas of my life.

These affirmations can help reinforce your commitment and dedication to your goals, empowering you to take consistent action and achieve the success you desire.

I am fully committed to achieving my goals and manifesting my dreams.

I dedicate myself wholeheartedly to the pursuit of success and excellence.

I embrace the journey towards my goals with passion, determination, and perseverance.

I am willing to do whatever it takes to achieve my dreams and create the life I desire.

I am focused and disciplined, channeling my energy into productive actions that move me closer to success.
I am relentless in my pursuit of greatness, refusing to settle for mediocrity or compromise my ambitions.

I am accountable for my own success and take full responsibility for my actions and outcomes.

I am committed to continuous growth and self-improvement, always striving to be better than I was yesterday.

I am resilient in the face of challenges and setbacks, using them as opportunities for growth and learning.

I am confident in my abilities and trust in my capacity to overcome any obstacles that may arise.

I am focused on the present moment, fully immersed in the tasks at hand and giving them my undivided attention.
I am proactive and resourceful, seeking out solutions and opportunities even in the face of adversity.

I am driven by a clear vision of success and am unwavering in my pursuit of that vision.

I am committed to taking consistent action towards my goals, knowing that every small step adds up to big progress over time.

I am disciplined in my habits and routines, ensuring that I prioritize activities that align with my goals and values.

I am unstoppable in my pursuit of success, and I refuse to let fear or doubt hold me back from achieving my dreams.

I am resilient in the face of obstacles, and I trust in my ability to overcome any challenges that come my way.
I am committed to my own growth and development, and I invest time and energy into learning and improving myself every day.

I am fully committed to my goals, and I am willing to put in the hard work and effort required to achieve them.

I am focused and determined, and I persevere through challenges with courage and resilience.

I am dedicated to my success, and I take consistent action towards my goals every single day.

I am resilient in the face of setbacks, and I use them as opportunities to learn and grow.

I am committed to achieving my dreams, and I am willing to do whatever it takes to make them a reality.
I am disciplined in my actions, and I stay focused on my goals even when faced with distractions or obstacles.

I am persistent in my pursuit of success, and I never give up on my dreams.

I am resourceful and creative, and I find solutions to any challenges that arise on my journey to success.

I am dedicated to my personal growth and development, and I invest time and energy into improving myself every day.

I am committed to my goals, and I take consistent action towards achieving them.

I am focused and determined, and I persevere through challenges with courage and resilience.

I am dedicated to my success, and I take consistent action towards my goals every single day.

I am resilient in the face of setbacks, and I use them as opportunities to learn and grow.

I am committed to achieving my dreams, and I am willing to do whatever it takes to make them a reality.

I am disciplined in my actions, and I stay focused on my goals even when faced with distractions or obstacles.

I am persistent in my pursuit of success, and I never give up on my dreams.

I am resourceful and creative, and I find solutions to any challenges that arise on my journey to success.
I am dedicated to my personal growth and development, and I invest time and energy into improving myself every day.

I am committed to my goals, and I take consistent action towards achieving them.

I am focused and determined, and I persevere through challenges with courage and resilience.

I am dedicated to my success, and I take consistent action towards my goals every single day.

I am resilient in the face of setbacks, and I use them as opportunities to learn and grow.

**These affirmations can help cultivate a
mindset of gratitude, opening your heart to
appreciate the abundance and blessings
that surround you each day.**

*I am grateful for the abundance that surrounds me in every
aspect of my life.*

*I appreciate the beauty of each moment and find joy in the
simplest of pleasures.*

*I am thankful for the love and support of my family and
friends, who enrich my life with their presence.*

*I express gratitude for the challenges I face, knowing that
they offer opportunities for growth and learning.*

*I am grateful for my health and well-being, cherishing the
gift of vitality and strength.*
*I give thanks for the abundance of opportunities that come
my way, seizing each one with enthusiasm and gratitude.*

*I am thankful for the abundance of nature, marveling at
the wonders of the world around me.*

*I express gratitude for the lessons learned from past
experiences, using them to guide me on my journey forward.*

*I am grateful for the wisdom of mentors and teachers who
have shared their knowledge and guidance with me.*

I appreciate the kindness and generosity of strangers, recognizing the interconnectedness of all beings.

I give thanks for the blessings of each new day, embracing the potential it holds for growth and transformation.
I am thankful for the opportunities to give back and make a positive impact in the lives of others.

I express gratitude for the abundance of love and compassion in my heart, which I share freely with those around me.

I am grateful for the gift of mindfulness, allowing me to fully experience each moment with presence and awareness.

I give thanks for the strength and resilience within me, which empower me to overcome any obstacle.

I appreciate the beauty of diversity and celebrate the unique gifts and talents of every individual.

I am grateful for the support of my community, which uplifts and sustains me on my journey.
I give thanks for the opportunity to learn and grow, embracing the challenges that lead to personal transformation.

I express gratitude for the abundance of creativity and inspiration that flows through me, fueling my passions and pursuits.

I am thankful for the gift of forgiveness, which frees me from the burden of resentment and bitterness.

I give thanks for the abundance of opportunities to connect with others and build meaningful relationships.

I am grateful for the power of laughter and joy, which uplift my spirit and lighten my heart.

I appreciate the beauty of each sunrise and sunset, reminding me of the cycle of renewal and rebirth.
I give thanks for the abundance of resources that support my journey and nourish my body, mind, and soul.

I express gratitude for the privilege of life itself, savoring each moment as a precious gift.

I am thankful for the abundance of possibilities that lie ahead, embracing the unknown with curiosity and excitement.

I give thanks for the strength and courage within me, which empower me to face challenges with resilience and grace.

I appreciate the blessings of peace and serenity, which fill my heart and soul with tranquility.

I am grateful for the gift of creativity, which allows me to express myself authentically and passionately.

I express gratitude for the abundance of love and connection in my life, which bring meaning and purpose to every day.

These declarations can help cultivate a mindset of gratitude towards money, recognizing its role in providing for essential needs and contributing to overall well-being. It's very important to always view money as positive energy. This simple notion attracts money to you. For example, rather than saying you" cannot believe the cost of groceries", change that perspective to something like, "thank you money for allowing me to feed my family". "I don't have money for this, I have to put it on my credit card!!", Changes to , "thank you for the ability to put this cost on to my credit card." Money should ALWAYS be spoken of as a positive. This is a fundamental law of attracting financial success. Every penny you have or every penny you may have to borrow, you should be greatful for.

I express gratitude to money for its abundant flow, allowing me to pay my bills with ease and grace.

I am thankful to money for providing me with the means to cover my expenses and meet my financial obligations. I appreciate the role of money in ensuring I have a roof over my head and food on my table.

I thank money for its ability to support me in meeting my basic needs and living a comfortable life.

I express deep gratitude to money for its consistent presence in my life, allowing me to provide for myself and my loved ones.

I acknowledge the blessings that money brings, enabling me to maintain a stable and secure lifestyle.

I am grateful to money for its role in ensuring I have access to necessary resources and services.

I thank money for its capacity to alleviate financial stress and provide me with peace of mind.
I appreciate money for its role in allowing me to enjoy the comforts and conveniences of daily life.

I express heartfelt gratitude to money for its unwavering support in meeting my financial needs and obligations.

These declarations can help cultivate a mindset of trust and surrender, allowing you to lean into the divine timing of God and the universe, and find peace in the knowledge that everything unfolds according to a higher plan.

I trust in the divine timing of God and the universe, knowing that all things unfold according to a higher plan.

I have faith that everything happens for a reason, and I surrender to the wisdom of divine timing.

I believe that God's timing is always perfect, and I patiently await the blessings that are destined to come my way.

I release the need to rush or force outcomes, trusting that the universe is orchestrating everything in divine order.
I accept that delays and detours are part of the journey, and I trust that they serve a greater purpose in my life.

I trust in the unfolding of divine timing, knowing that it holds the keys to my highest good and greatest fulfillment.

I surrender my desires to the wisdom of the universe, trusting that what is meant for me will never miss me.

I have faith that the universe is always conspiring in my favor, even when things don't go according to my plans.

I release the need to control outcomes and instead surrender to the flow of divine timing.

I trust that the universe has a plan for me, and I embrace each moment with gratitude and acceptance.

These declarations can help shift your mindset away from negativity and towards positivity, allowing you to see the beauty and abundance that exists in every situation.

I choose to see the good in every situation, no matter how challenging it may seem.

I release negative thoughts and embrace positivity in all aspects of my life.

I am grateful for the lessons learned from difficult situations and choose to focus on the positive outcomes.

I attract positivity into my life by maintaining a mindset of gratitude and optimism.

I let go of negativity and replace it with thoughts of love, abundance, and joy.
I find beauty and blessings in every experience, even those that may initially appear negative.

I trust that everything happens for my highest good, and I choose to see the silver lining in every situation.

I am the master of my thoughts, and I choose to focus on the positive aspects of life.

I cultivate an attitude of gratitude, finding reasons to be thankful in every moment.

I shift my perspective to one of positivity and abundance, knowing that my thoughts shape my reality.

I release resistance and welcome positivity and abundance into my life with open arms.
I am surrounded by blessings and opportunities, and I choose to see them in every situation.

I let go of judgment and criticism, choosing instead to see the good in myself and others.

I am a beacon of positivity, spreading love and light wherever I go.

I celebrate the beauty of life and appreciate the abundance that surrounds me.

I release the need to dwell on negativity and focus instead on the abundance of positivity in my life.

I embrace each day with a heart full of gratitude and a mind filled with positivity.

I choose to see challenges as opportunities for growth and transformation.

I am grateful for the abundance of blessings in my life, both big and small.

I radiate positivity and attract positive experiences into my life effortlessly.

POLOTICS, INFLATION, CORRUPTTION, SOCIAL ANXIETY, SOCIAL MEDIA, NEGATIVE PRESS, HATE, NONE OF THIS IS YOUR CONCERN.

These declarations can help redirect your focus towards what truly matters—self-care, meaningful relationships, and personal growth—while empowering you to make positive choices that contribute to your own well-being and the well-being of those around you.

I release worry about external circumstances and focus my energy on cultivating inner peace and contentment.

I detach from negative politics, authority, and social media, and instead prioritize my well-being and the well-being of my loved ones.

I choose to focus on what I can control, knowing that my choices have the power to shape my reality.

I let go of the need to change the world around me and instead focus on changing myself for the better.
I cultivate a sense of gratitude for the blessings in my life and the relationships that bring me joy and fulfillment.

I recognize that I cannot control external events, but I can control how I respond to them with grace and resilience.

I release fear and anxiety about the state of the world and trust in my ability to navigate challenges with strength and courage.

I prioritize self-care and self-love, knowing that by taking care of myself, I am better able to support those around me.

I surround myself with positivity and love, distancing myself from negativity and toxic influences.

I focus on fostering meaningful connections with family and friends, cherishing the moments we share together.

I choose to be a beacon of light and positivity in the world, spreading kindness and compassion wherever I go.

I release the need for external validation and instead find validation within myself and my own sense of worth.

I trust in the power of my own choices to create positive change in my life and the lives of those around me.

I let go of comparison and competition, focusing instead on my own journey of growth and self-discovery.

I embrace the present moment with gratitude and mindfulness, savoring the beauty of life's simple pleasures.

I release the burden of trying to control outcomes and instead surrender to the flow of life, trusting in the divine timing of the universe.

I prioritize my mental and emotional well-being, setting boundaries to protect myself from negativity and stress.

I let go of the need for perfection and embrace my imperfections as part of what makes me uniquely human.

I focus on living authentically and aligning my actions with my values and beliefs.

I choose to focus on love, hope, and positivity, knowing that my attitude has the power to influence the world around me.

~~THE END~~

Actually

Its

THE BEGINNING!

GREAT THINGS WILL HAPPEN!

YOU ARE BLESSED ALREADY!

Share them using the **#BATHFIRMATIONS**
hash tag!

Ps. If this is a bathroom reader, one last affirmation.

I CHOOSE TO WASH MY HANDS

Use these pages to write down your favorite affirmations or affirmations of your own.

_____

_____

_____

_____

_____

_____

_____

_____

_____

_____

_____

_____

_____

_____

_____

_____

_____

_____

_____

_____

_____